Original title:
Aurora Reflections

Copyright © 2024 Swan Charm
All rights reserved.

Author: Olivia Orav
ISBN HARDBACK: 978-9908-52-665-2
ISBN PAPERBACK: 978-9908-52-666-9
ISBN EBOOK: 978-9908-52-667-6

The Spectrum of Morning Chants

The sun peeks through the trees,
With laughter in the air,
Colors dance on blooming leaves,
A joyous fire we share.

Birds sing sweet melodies,
As flowers sway in rhyme,
Morning's canvas paints the scene,
In beauty, lost in time.

Crisp and fresh the morning breeze,
Whispers of delight,
Footsteps follow in the cheer,
As day breaks into light.

With smiles bright and hearts aglow,
We gather hand in hand,
The spectrum wraps our spirits high,
In this enchanted land.

Ephemeral Skies Unveiled

Beneath the twinkling stars so bright,
We dance beneath the moonlit light.
Joy weaves through the evening air,
With laughter echoing everywhere.

The fireworks paint the velvet night,
In bursts of color, pure delight.
Together we embrace the thrill,
In this moment, time stands still.

Daybreak's Quiet Contemplations

Morning whispers through the haze,
Golden beams ignite the days.
With coffee cups raised high in cheer,
We gather close, friends that are dear.

Birds sing sweetly in the trees,
Carrying tales upon the breeze.
The world awakens, soft and warm,
In this stillness, hearts are born.

The Jewels of Dusk

As day transforms to twilight's hue,
We gather round with joys anew.
The sky adorned with crimson glow,
Each moment shared begins to flow.

Candles flicker, shadows dance,
In every gaze, a sweet romance.
The stars emerge, their light sublime,
We weave our dreams, transcending time.

Flickers of Transcendence

In gatherings rich with laughter's sound,
The spirit of joy is profoundly found.
We share our hopes, our wishes bright,
As flickers of dreams take to flight.

With hearts united, we embrace,
This tapestry of love and grace.
Each moment precious, like a song,
In festivity, we all belong.

Celestial Reverie in Twilight

Stars awaken, the sky aglow,
Colors blend in a splendid show.
Whispers of laughter fill the air,
As dreams and hopes rise, free from care.

Lanterns float on gentle streams,
Illuminating our wildest dreams.
Joyous songs from hearts so bright,
A symphony of love in the night.

Awakening the Silent Spectrum

Dawn paints the world in hues anew,
Emerging light, a radiant view.
Petals dance in the morning breeze,
Nature's canvas, meant to please.

Bees buzz sweetly between the blooms,
A joyful chorus in the glooms.
Every heartbeat, a vibrant line,
In this moment, we intertwine.

A Symphony of Colors Breaking

Sunset splashes the horizon wide,
Crimson waves on an evening tide.
Choruses rise in the fading light,
Celebrating the magic of night.

Fires flicker in the gathering spell,
Stories dance in a vibrant swell.
Under the stars, we take our place,
Unity found in this space.

The Dance of Light and Shadow

Moonlight glimmers on the silver lake,
Each ripple tells of dreams awake.
The night unfolds its shimmering veil,
In the softest whispers, our hopes sail.

Together we weave a tapestry grand,
In this glorious, enchanted land.
With laughter and warmth, let us ignite,
The dance of our hearts in the night.

Dawn's Gentle Mirages

A golden hue paints the sky,
Laughter dances, as children fly.
The flowers bloom, bright and bold,
Whispers of joy, stories told.

Sunlight glistens on the dew,
Every heartbeat feels brand new.
Nature sings in sweet refrain,
Weaving dreams like gentle rain.

Banners wave, the town alive,
Where every heart starts to thrive.
Bubbles rise with every cheer,
Echoes of love, drawing near.

The Pulsing Light

Underneath the twinkling stars,
The night pulses with vibrant bars.
Drums beat heavy, feet align,
In this moment, all is divine.

Colors swirl in cosmic spin,
As friends gather, smiles within.
The air buzzes with delight,
A celebration of pure light.

Candles flicker, shadows play,
Laughter guides us, come what may.
In every shadow, joy is sought,
Together we weave the moments caught.

The Poetry of the Universe

Stars whisper secrets in the night,
Galaxies dance, a wondrous sight.
In the silence, hearts take flight,
Crafting dreams in shared delight.

The moon beams down, soft like silk,
Filling our souls with magic milk.
Every breath, a stanza sweet,
Where love and laughter gently meet.

The cosmos hums, a timeless song,
Reminding us where we belong.
In this vast and vibrant space,
We find our rhythm, we find our grace.

Celestial Reveries

Amidst the stars, we gather round,
In every glance, connection found.
With every wish upon a star,
We dream of wonders near and far.

Fireflies twinkle in the air,
Their magic whispers everywhere.
Hands held tight, we share the spark,
Illuminating the dusky dark.

Voices rise in joyful song,
In this moment, we all belong.
With open hearts, we chase the dream,
In celestial realms, we beam.

Elysian Glow at Daybreak

Golden rays break through the trees,
Dancing leaves in gentle breeze.
Birds sing sweet, their morning song,
In this moment, all feels strong.

Petals bloom in colors bright,
Waking hearts with pure delight.
Joyful whispers fill the air,
Nature's gift, beyond compare.

Nature's Light Mosaic

Vibrant hues spread wide and free,
Nature paints a tapestry.
Butterflies flit here and there,
In the sun, without a care.

Rivers sparkle, laughter flows,
Where the gentle breeze bestows.
Every creature joins the dance,
In this wild, enchanting trance.

The Sky's Silent Serenade

Clouds drift softly, cotton white,
Stars awaken with the night.
Moonlight spills like silver dew,
Whispers secrets, old and new.

Crickets chirp in harmony,
Nature's grand symphony.
In the stillness, dreams take flight,
Underneath the soothing night.

Transcendence at Day's Embrace

Dawn unfolds with glowing grace,
Morning wraps us in its embrace.
Hope ignites with every ray,
At the start of this new day.

Children laugh, their spirits soar,
All together, we explore.
Hand in hand, we chase the light,
In this world, our hearts unite.

Luminous Secrets of Daybreak

The dawn awakens with a cheerful glow,
Soft whispers of light on the hills below.
Joy dances in hues, vibrant and bold,
As daybreak's embrace turns darkness to gold.

Birds sing in chorus, a jubilant song,
Welcoming warmth where shadows once throng.
The world is renewed, a canvas so bright,
Unveiling its beauty with pure delight.

Echoes of the Radiant Horizon

On the horizon, colors gleam and play,
A symphony of light heralding the day.
Golden rays stretch out, embracing the earth,
With every new dawn, there's promise, rebirth.

Laughter resounds, echoing the morn,
As gathered together, new joys are born.
The sky smiles bright, a jubilant expanse,
Inviting us all to join in the dance.

Veil of Night's Resurgence

The twilight descends with a gentle flair,
Stars twinkle above, shimmering in air.
Festive dreams rise with the moon's embrace,
As whispers of night unveil a soft grace.

Lanterns glow warmly, a comforting sight,
In celebration, we gather this night.
Voices entwine in a melodious hum,
As the pulse of the evening beckons us come.

Celestial Brushstrokes at Dawn

The sky is a canvas, painted with light,
Brushstrokes of amber chase away the night.
A wondrous display, as wonders arise,
In festive colors, the world shall surprise.

With laughter and joy filling the air,
Hearts beat as one in a moment so rare.
Nature's own feast, a glorious scene,
As we bask together, in harmony's sheen.

The First Light's Promise

With morning's glow, dreams take flight,
Joy dances in the soft daylight.
Colors burst, the world awakes,
In this moment, the heart remakes.

Laughter fills the vibrant air,
Promises linger without a care.
Children play, their spirits bright,
A symphony of pure delight.

Nature sings in brilliant hues,
Each petal kissed with morning dew.
In every smile, hope ignites,
The day unfurls its endless lights.

Twilight's Whispered Secrets

As daylight fades, stars appear,
Magic stirs, the night is near.
Shadows dance on silver streams,
In twilight's glow, we share our dreams.

The breeze carries soft, sweet tunes,
Lifting hearts like bright balloons.
Together here in whispered grace,
The universe, our cherished space.

Candles flicker in warm embrace,
A tapestry of love we trace.
Every glance, a story told,
In twilight's charm, our hearts unfold.

Serenade of the Night Sky

Underneath the starry dome,
We gather close, away from home.
The moonlight spills like silver lace,
Enchanting all with its soft embrace.

Melodies drift on midnight air,
Every note a tender prayer.
Hearts entwined, we find our rhyme,
Through the dark, we chase the sublime.

The night is young, the spirit free,
A serenade for you and me.
In whispered dreams, we'll laugh and sing,
Together, we will spark the spring.

Luminous Echoes

Beneath the canopy of night,
Dreams ignite in pure delight.
Every glimmer, a wish we share,
Luminous echoes fill the air.

Dancing flames, our stories flow,
In this moment, together we glow.
Friendship blooms under the stars,
No distance can dim our hearts' memoirs.

With laughter bright, we fill the night,
Creating magic, a wondrous sight.
In the silence, joy is born,
With each heartbeat, a new dawn.

Dreams on the Horizon

Balloons drift high, colors so bright,
Laughter and joy fill the warm night.
Children dance under the twinkling lights,
Whispers of magic, delightful sights.

Candles aglow, casting their charms,
Friends gather close, wrapped in their arms.
The music floats softly, a sweet serenade,
Dreams take flight in this joyous parade.

Echoes of a Radiant Sky

Stars sparkle like diamonds in the deep,
Echoes of laughter, secrets we keep.
Fireflies weave through the breezy air,
Moments like these, so precious and rare.

With every cheer, our spirits unite,
Under the glow of the moon's silver light.
Cheers clink together, voices resound,
In this vibrant world, true bliss can be found.

Celestial Dance of Colors

Painted skies greet the dawning day,
Nature's palette, in bright array.
Costumes twirl in the summer's embrace,
Every smile etched on each joyous face.

The rhythm of drums sets hearts ablaze,
Fingers snap softly in colorful sways.
A tapestry woven with laughter and dreams,
Life's endless festival, bursting at seams.

Luminous Tapestry

Bright ribbons stream like the festival's heart,
Each small moment, a cherished part.
Voices harmonizing in sweet delight,
As shadows dance under stars so bright.

From dusk until dawn, in joyous cheer,
We gather together, with loved ones near.
In a luminous tapestry, we find our way,
Creating memories, brightening the day.

Canvas of Celestial Visions

Bright fireworks light the night,
Colors dance in joyful flight.
Laughter echoes, hearts embrace,
In this wondrous, vibrant space.

Banners sway in the gentle breeze,
Whispers of joy among the trees.
Families gather, spirits high,
Underneath the starlit sky.

Music flows like a river wide,
People join in with pride.
Voices mingle, sweet refrain,
Together we forget our pain.

As shadows fade, the dawn will break,
Memories linger, hearts awake.
A canvas painted with delight,
Festive dreams in colors bright.

Chromatic Burst of Hope

Sunrise spills its golden light,
Painting pathways, visions bright.
Colors splash on every face,
A festival, a warm embrace.

Balloon animals drift up high,
Giggles weave through the blue sky.
Everyone joins the merry sway,
As laughter dances through the day.

Bubbles float in joyful glee,
Spectacles of harmony.
Hope ignites like fireworks wide,
Echoing love, our hearts collide.

In this burst, we find our way,
A radiant path, come what may.
With every smile, the world feels new,
Festive hearts, together we grew.

Serene Dusk Whispers

As daylight bids a soft goodbye,
Stars emerge to light the sky.
Candles flicker, shadows play,
Welcoming night, the end of day.

Joyful songs drift through the air,
With each note, we shed our care.
Peace surrounds us, warm and bright,
In this moment, pure delight.

Laughter mingles with the breeze,
Moments shared beneath the trees.
Stories told with gentle grace,
Memories forged in this embrace.

Underneath the twilight glow,
A serene hush begins to flow.
In this stillness, hearts align,
Festive spirits forever shine.

Dreamscapes Beneath the Stars

Sweet dreams linger in the night,
Starlit canvas, pure delight.
Whirls of magic fill the air,
As we gather without a care.

Fireflies twinkle, soft and bright,
Casting spells in the velvet night.
With every glance, a wish is made,
Dreamscapes bloom in the night shade.

Voices rise in harmony,
Each note holds a memory.
Here we dance, the world feels right,
In these moments, our hearts ignite.

As constellations twinkle high,
We weave our dreams into the sky.
In joy, we find our sweetest rest,
A festive night, forever blessed.

Spheres of Light in Tranquil Air

Twinkling stars in velvet skies,
Joining hands as night-time sighs.
Laughter dances on the breeze,
Whispers soft 'neath swaying trees.

Lanterns glow with warm embrace,
Each flicker tells a tale of grace.
Joyful hearts in harmony,
In this realm, we're wild and free.

Canvas of Dreams in the Firmament

Colors burst in twilight's fold,
Stories written, bright and bold.
Brushstrokes paint the evening air,
Magic glimmers everywhere.

Voices blend like songs of spring,
Every note a joyful fling.
Underneath this cosmic dome,
We create a world called home.

The Horizon's Gleaming Witness

As the sun begins to rise,
Golden hues light up the skies.
Shadows fade, and joy reborn,
Promises of a brand new morn.

Each heartbeat, a rhythmic cheer,
Gathered souls, drawing near.
Together, we can make a stand,
With our dreams, hand in hand.

Illuminated Whispers of Dawn

Morning dew like diamonds bright,
Nature wakes, a lovely sight.
Birdsong floats on gentle tides,
In this cheer where love abides.

Radiance bathes the waking earth,
Celebration, joy, and mirth.
Every heartbeat sings aloud,
We embrace the day, so proud.

Shadows Retreating with the Light

In the glow of the morning sun,
Shadows flee, the day's begun.
Colors dance on the soft dew,
A canvas bright, a world anew.

Laughter rings through the warm breeze,
Joy abounds, the heart's at ease.
Flowers bloom in vibrant cheer,
Nature sings, the time is near.

Children play with glee and light,
Chasing dreams in pure delight.
Every moment feels so right,
As shadows retreat with the light.

The Dawn's Melodic Lullaby

Softly hums the dawn's sweet song,
Birds join in, they all belong.
Morning whispers in hues so bright,
The world awakens, pure delight.

Gentle breezes twist and twine,
Nature's rhythm, so divine.
With each note, joy does arise,
Underneath the waking skies.

The sun stretches, yawns so wide,
Bathing all in golden tide.
Life unfolds in vibrant hue,
As dawn sings its lullaby true.

Dawn's Woven Dreams

Threads of pink and gold entwine,
In the sky where dreams align.
Morning whispers secrets bright,
Weaving tales of pure delight.

Each soft cloud, a story spun,
Glowing softly with the sun.
Radiant hues, a canvas wide,
Nature's beauty, joy and pride.

The world stirs with a gentle sigh,
As laughter dances, spirits fly.
In this tapestry of light,
Dawn's woven dreams take flight.

Whispers of the Northern Light

Under stars, the cold winds sing,
Whispers of magic, hearts take wing.
Sky aflame with a vibrant glow,
Auroras dance, a mesmerizing show.

Fires crackle, laughter resounds,
Joyful echoes in night's bounds.
Neighbors gather, share a smile,
Together in this festive style.

The northern light, a wondrous sight,
Filling souls with pure delight.
Together we hold this night dear,
Whispers of joy, we all cheer.

Harmonic Glimmers

Beneath the stars, the laughter rings,
Dancing lights on joyous wings.
Melodies weave through the cool night air,
A vibrant pulse, hearts laid bare.

Candles flicker, colors burst,
In every moment, a jubilant thirst.
Faces bright with smiles and cheer,
Together we sing, the world feels near.

Glimmers of hope shine soft and bright,
In harmony, we embrace the night.
Hands held tightly, spirits soar,
Each heartbeat echoes, forevermore.

The festive night wraps us in bliss,
In this warm glow, we find pure happiness.
With every laugh, our souls entwine,
In harmonic glimmers, we perfectly shine.

Through the Eyes of the Cosmos

Starlit skies abound with dreams,
Galaxies twirl in radiant beams.
Through the eyes of the cosmos vast,
Time stands still, moments amassed.

Joyful whispers dance on the breeze,
Infinite wonders bring us to our knees.
Waves of light in swirling flight,
Invite us to revel in the night.

Ribbons of cosmos ignite the soul,
Filling our hearts, making us whole.
Celestial laughter wraps around,
In the cosmic embrace, love is found.

Each twinkle a wish, a secret shared,
A universe alive where none are spared.
Through the eyes of the cosmos, we see,
A boundless joy, forever free.

Shades of Awakening

In the dawn's glow, the colors breathe,
Shades of awakening, a world we weave.
Nature's palette bursts into play,
An artist's dream at break of day.

Through verdant fields, we wander wide,
Every moment a thrilling ride.
Soft melodies drift with the sun,
In shades of awakening, life's begun.

Laughter echoes through trees so tall,
In harmony, we rise, we fall.
Moments painted in joy divine,
In every heartbeat, the world aligns.

As petals bloom in joyful dance,
We lose ourselves in every chance.
Together we thrive in vibrant hues,
In shades of awakening, we find our muse.

The Brush of the Universe

With a brush dipped in stardust glow,
The universe paints, its wonders flow.
Each stroke a story, vibrant and bright,
Colors unfurl in the canvas of night.

Galaxies swirl like a wild dream,
A cosmic dance, an endless stream.
The brush of the universe spins the tales,
Of laughter and joy that never pales.

As constellations waltz in the sky,
We join the rhythm, hearts lifted high.
In every hue, a message profound,
In the brush of the universe, love is found.

Festive spirits take to the air,
In this grand masterpiece, we share.
Together we sing and paint our yore,
In the brush of the universe, forevermore.

Dancing Under Fading Stars

The night is alive, laughter so bright,
We sway with the breeze, lost in delight.
Each twinkle above, a whisper of cheer,
In this moment of joy, bring everyone near.

The world is our stage, the moon is our guide,
With hearts intertwined, we let love decide.
As shadows retreat, and dawn starts to play,
In this festive glow, we dance till the day.

Veils of Dawn

The morning unfolds with colors aglow,
Whispers of magic, in rays soft and slow.
With feet on the grass, we gather in cheer,
Come join this celebration, for songs we all hear.

Each petal that opens, tells tales of delight,
The sun climbs the sky, washing shadows in light.
In this vibrant moment, our spirits arise,
Veils of the dawn, painted across the skies.

Celestial Serenade

Stars gather round, in a shimmering grace,
The night hums a tune, inviting embrace.
Voices of euphoria, blend with the night,
In this celestial dance, everything feels right.

With the moon as a witness, we sing and we sway,
Together united, come what may.
Each note is a gift, wrapped in love's glow,
In this festive serenade, let all spirits flow.

Illuminated Horizons

The horizon ignites with a golden hue,
Faces aglow, a radiant view.
We gather like fireflies, lighting the scene,
In the warmth of this moment, we share a dream.

With laughter like music, we leap and we spin,
In a world full of wonder, where joy can begin.
As the sky drapes in colors so bold,
In illuminated horizons, our stories unfold.

Dawn's Ethereal Dance

A crisp breeze sweeps the waking land,
Sunbeams twirl, a golden band.
Birds chirp sweet, a cheerful tune,
Morning smiles beneath the moon.

Flowers bloom in joyous sway,
Nature's canvas, bright display.
Laughter dances on the air,
Happiness is everywhere.

Colors of the Awakening Sky

Crimson blushes greet the dawn,
Blue and gold, a canvas drawn.
Soft pastels spread like dreams,
Nature bursts with vibrant schemes.

Joyful chants from trees above,
Hearts are light, in peace, we love.
Clouds adorned in shades so bright,
Celebrate the day, pure delight.

Whispers Beneath the Northern Lights

Emerald beams across the night,
Stars shimmer, a wondrous sight.
In the silence, voices glide,
Magic flows like a gentle tide.

Dancing shadows start to play,
Underneath the skies' ballet.
Hope ignites in every heart,
From this beauty, we won't part.

Celestial Tapestry Unfurled

Glistening threads of starlit hue,
Weaving dreams, a cosmic view.
The universe hums a joyful song,
In this realm, we all belong.

Colors whirl, a grand embrace,
In this moment, we find our place.
Together under the endless sky,
With every laugh, we soar high.

Serenity Beneath the Shimmering Veil

Underneath the stars that gleam,
Whispers dance in gentle streams.
A night of joy, a tale unfolds,
In dreams of peace, our hearts behold.

Lanterns sway with soft delight,
Filling shadows with warm light.
Gathered round, we share our song,
In this moment, we belong.

Laughter rings like silver bells,
Echoes weaving vibrant spells.
Beneath the moon's enchanting grace,
We find our warmth, our sacred space.

As twilight wraps us in its cheer,
Every smile, every whisper near.
Together woven, heart to heart,
In this serenity, we part.

Chasing the First Light

At dawn the world begins to gleam,
Chasing shadows, waking dreams.
A splash of gold bursts through the trees,
With every moment, joyful breeze.

The bustle starts, the day awakes,
Coffee brews and laughter shakes.
With open arms, we greet the day,
In fiery hues that softly play.

Every face a canvas bright,
With smiles that bring a spark of light.
Together we embrace anew,
Finding joy in all we do.

As sunlight spills across the land,
We weave our dreams with gentle hands.
In every heartbeat, every glance,
Life invites us to this dance.

Dreaming in Pastels

Soft brush strokes of rosy hue,
Painting skies in morning dew.
Whispers of a world so sweet,
In pastel dreams, our hearts repeat.

Petals fall like tender sighs,
Coloring the earth and skies.
Every moment feels like song,
In this lovely, vibrant throng.

Children play, their laughter bright,
Joyful dances in pure light.
As the sun dips low and warm,
We find magic in the calm.

With every shade, we come alive,
In the whispers of dreams, we thrive.
Together woven in life's art,
In pastel hues, we share our heart.

The Light that Paints the Sky

As day surrenders to the night,
The sky ignites with colors bright.
A canvas brushed with fiery dreams,
Where hope and wonder dance in beams.

Stars emerge in twinkling grace,
Filling time and empty space.
With every twirl of light above,
We celebrate our bond of love.

With every pulse, the world awakes,
In golden glows and gentle shakes.
The magic weaves through every soul,
Lighting paths that make us whole.

So raise your glass, let spirits soar,
In joyful cheers, let's want for more.
Together under this vast sky,
We revel in the reasons why.

Shimmers of Secret Skies

Stars twinkle in the velvet vast,
Whispers dance on a gentle breeze,
Glistening lights from shadows cast,
In the night, the heart feels at ease.

Flashes of laughter paint the air,
Colors of joy in every glance,
Moments captured, all can share,
In this realm, the world's a dance.

Mirrors of dreams beneath the glow,
Sparkling stories, tales untold,
Underneath the sparkling show,
Lies a treasure more than gold.

As the night wraps in its embrace,
With every shimmer, spirits rise,
In this enchanting, lively space,
We celebrate the secret skies.

A Palette of the Ethereal

Brushstrokes of laughter paint the night,
With hues that shimmer, dance, and play,
Joyful echoes take their flight,
In this canvas, hearts sway.

Colors burst like fireworks bright,
Each moment a brush with delight,
Spirits lifted, soaring high,
Under the moon's watchful eye.

Whirls of dreams in pastel seas,
As the night releases its charms,
We gather close with joyful ease,
Wrapped in warmth, safe in each other's arms.

A symphony of stars aligns,
In the silence, music sings,
Brush away the daily lines,
In this realm, pure magic springs.

Secrets of the Night Sky

In the stillness, secrets bloom,
Stars unfurl their hidden tales,
Softly cradling the night's soft room,
As the moonlight gently exhales.

Whispers weave through the twilight air,
Each flicker holds a cherished dream,
A tapestry of hope laid bare,
As the world dances in a gleam.

Silver threads of laughter rise,
Spinning joy from shadows deep,
In the embrace of starlit skies,
We harvest memories to keep.

Together we weave our lives anew,
In this festive, radiant night,
Guided by the cosmic hue,
Chasing wonders in shared light.

The Language of Light

In rays of amber, stories unfold,
Cascading warmth around our hearts,
A silent language, gentle and bold,
Where each glance a masterpiece starts.

Glistening laughter spills like wine,
Brightening shadows that linger near,
Moments glowing, a perfect design,
Crafted with love, wrapped in cheer.

Echoes of joy through the night air,
Painting the universe in delight,
Each spark a wish, a heartfelt prayer,
In the vibrant embrace of light.

Together we bask in this shine,
A symphony of colors so bright,
In the closeness, our spirits intertwine,
Speaking softly in the language of light.

Dayspring's Quirks

With laughter sweet, the morn unfolds,
Bright ribbons dance, in colors bold.
Joy spills forth from every nook,
As sunbeams play, the world's a book.

Chasing shadows, light takes flight,
Balloons ascend to greet the night.
With friends beside, we spin and twirl,
A festive whirl, our spirits swirl.

Laughter echoes in the air,
As petals drift, we dance with flair.
The joy of living fills the day,
In every heart, the spark will stay.

So raise a toast to dawn's bright cheer,
In every smile, the love is clear.
Together here, let warm hearts sing,
For every day, a joyful spring.

Stratified Skies of Imagination

Upon the clouds, our dreams take flight,
Pastel shades glow in morning light.
With laughter bright, we paint the air,
In vibrant hues, we banish care.

Kites unfurl in a dance with breeze,
We chase our wishes among the trees.
A tapestry of hope and cheer,
The magic of our day is here.

Amidst the laughter, stories bloom,
In every corner, joy finds room.
With visions wild, we roam so free,
In this grand world of jubilee.

So let's embark on this delight,
Where dreams take wing, and hearts ignite.
With every glance, a spark we share,
In skies of wonder, we declare.

The Art of Celestial Transitions

As day gives way to starry night,
The moon reveals her silver light.
We gather close, our dreams unite,
In this embrace, pure hearts take flight.

The twinkling stars, a wink, a dance,
Inviting us to take a chance.
With whispered tales of love and cheer,
We weave the magic, crystal clear.

From dusk to dawn, the colors merge,
In rhythmic waves, our spirits surge.
With every breath, we craft delight,
As shadows bow to morning bright.

So let us drift on this sweet breeze,
Embrace the changes, hearts at ease.
In every moment, joy ignites,
In cosmic dance, our love takes flight.

Drift of the Ethereal Muse

In realms of dreams, where fairies play,
Whispers of joy light up the day.
With every spark, our spirits gleam,
Caught in the glow of friendship's beam.

As petals swirl in evening's glow,
We dance like rivers, free to flow.
The laughter shared, a precious tune,
Under the watchful eyes of the moon.

Each moment glistens, pure and bright,
In the embrace of warmth and light.
Together we'll chase the fleeting bliss,
In every hug, a world of kiss.

So let us gather, hand in hand,
In this enchanted, vibrant land.
With hearts aflame and spirits high,
We drift in love, beneath the sky.

Radiance in the Shadows

In the glow of lantern light,
Laughter dances, hearts take flight.
Whispers soft, like a sweet tune,
Joy unfolds beneath the moon.

Colors bright in every hand,
As we gather, dreams expand.
Sparkling eyes and warm embrace,
Festive spirits fill the space.

With each smile, the night ignites,
Magic weaves through joyful sights.
Stories shared, our voices blend,
In this moment, love transcends.

Under stars, we sway and sing,
Joyful echoes, the night we bring.
Radiant hearts, forever true,
In shadows bright, we find our cue.

When Night Meets Day

As the twilight softly fades,
Colors blend, a dance cascades.
Whispers rise with gentle cheer,
In this moment, all are near.

Golden rays meet silver night,
Each heartbeat echoes pure delight.
Joyous laughter fills the air,
As dreams float softly everywhere.

Candles flicker, spirits soar,
Every step, we yearn for more.
In this union, time stands still,
Hearts entwined, a gentle thrill.

Hand in hand, we greet the dawn,
In between the dusk and morn.
As night yields to the day's embrace,
Together, we will find our place.

Illuminations of the Heart

Beneath the stars, we come alive,
In shared warmth, our spirits strive.
Each flicker tells a tale of old,
In glowing tones, our dreams unfold.

Songs of joy rise through the air,
Gathered close, without a care.
Every heartbeat, every laugh,
We weave together, our own path.

With lanterns bright, we light the way,
Creating magic in our play.
In this circle, love shines true,
Festive hearts, forever new.

Memories dance with every tear,
Celebration whispers near.
In the glow of friendship's start,
We find our light, illuminations of the heart.

Colors of the Whispering Sky

Underneath a canvas bright,
Colors swirl, a pure delight.
Every brushstroke, laughter flows,
In the sky, our spirit glows.

With every shade, we weave our tale,
Through gentle breezes, hopes set sail.
A tapestry of friendship's thread,
In the light, no fear or dread.

As the sun dips below the line,
We gather close, a heart entwined.
In this moment, dreams collide,
Festive souls, we walk with pride.

With every hue, our hearts ignite,
In the whispers of the night.
Colors bright against the dark,
Together, we create the spark.

Tints of Tranquility

Balloons dance in the sun,
Colors bright, laughter spun.
Sweet cakes and cheerful song,
With friends where we belong.

Jubilant hearts comingle,
In a world where joys tingle.
Stars twinkle in twilight's embrace,
Every moment, a warm trace.

Candles flicker, stories unfold,
Whispers of love, tenderly told.
A tapestry of dreams tonight,
Underneath the soft moonlight.

Champagne bubbles rise high,
As wishes on the breeze fly.
Here's to laughter and cheer,
In tranquility, we draw near.

Secrets Carried by the Wind

Whispers of joy through the trees,
Gentle tunes ride the breeze.
Colors blur in the playful spins,
The laughter of children begins.

Garlands swirl, the night ignites,
Stars shimmer, delicate lights.
With every gust, secrets float,
On waves of joy, we all gloat.

The air alive with song and cheer,
Every heart's wish is near.
Dancing shadows find their way,
In the magic of this day.

Tales of old, new dreams start,
In the wind, they twine apart.
Festive spirits soar and rise,
While laughter paints the skies.

Reflections in a Celestial Mirror

Underneath the azure sphere,
Dreams reflect, crystal clear.
Festive lights in every glance,
As we waltz in a joyous dance.

Fireflies flicker, laughter echoes,
In the night, soft magic flows.
Every smile, a radiant beam,
In this lively, vibrant dream.

Moments cherished, time stands still,
Songs of happiness to fulfill.
With every wink, the stars align,
In this realm where spirits shine.

Sparks of joy ignite the night,
In harmony, our hearts take flight.
A celestial mirror, bright and bold,
Reflecting wonders yet untold.

The Metaphor of Light

Candles flicker, shadows play,
Embers dance through the fray.
Golden beams on smiling faces,
In joy, the heart embraces.

With every spark, a story glows,
In the warmth, our friendship grows.
We gather close, sharing delight,
Wrapped in the metaphor of light.

Jubilant rhythms fill the air,
With laughter woven everywhere.
Colors burst in joyous sight,
As we bask in this sheer light.

Together we shine, love's embrace,
Creating magic, weaving grace.
This festive glow, a heart's invite,
Forever warmed by love's pure light.

Celestial Kaleidoscope

Stars twinkle in the night,
Colors dancing, oh so bright.
Laughter echoes through the air,
Joy is swirling everywhere.

Underneath the moon's warm glow,
Magic bursts, a radiant show.
Children play with hearts so free,
Dreams unfurl like flowers, see!

Confetti falls in joyous flurry,
Time stands still; there's no hurry.
Together we weave our delight,
In this wondrous, colorful night.

With every moment, spirits soar,
Embracing all we can explore.
Life's a canvas, painted wide,
In this kaleidoscope, we glide.

Chasing Ethereal Veils

Glimmers of light weave and sway,
Colors mingle, night turns to day.
Whispers of joy upon the breeze,
Bring forth laughter, hearts at ease.

Shimmering fabrics drape the ground,
In this realm, peace can be found.
Dancing shadows come alive,
Magic rises, we will thrive.

Stars above like jewels bright,
Guide our steps this festive night.
In a tapestry spun with grace,
Every smile, a warm embrace.

Chasing veils of dreams untold,
In this moment, hearts behold.
Life's a festival, bright and grand,
Together, we will always stand.

The Symphony of Colors

Crimson blooms in the gentle breeze,
Hues of orange rustle the trees.
Golden rays kiss the earth anew,
In every shade, joy breaks through.

Dancing figures paint the scene,
Each connection, a joyful dream.
Rhythms pulse through the evening light,
Our spirits lifting, taking flight.

Flavors mingle, each taste a song,
In this moment, we all belong.
Voices rise, harmonies unite,
Celebrating life, love, and light.

A symphony crafted with care,
Notes of laughter fill the air.
Hand in hand, we weave the night,
In colorful echoes, pure delight.

Twilight's Embrace

Twilight casts its gentle hue,
Soft whispers call, they lead us through.
In the dusk, magic seems to glow,
Where shadows dance, our dreams can flow.

Lanterns flicker, hearts ignite,
Bringing warmth to the cool night.
Every glimmer tells a story,
Of laughter shared, of fleeting glory.

The air is filled with sweet perfume,
In the twilight, colors bloom.
With friends beside, we raise our cheer,
Embracing moments precious, dear.

As night unfolds its starry quilt,
We gather close, our worries wilt.
In twilight's embrace, we find our place,
Lost in time, a joyous space.

When Colors Collide at Dawn

The sun peeks shyly, painting skies,
With strokes of pink and orange rise.
As laughter dances in the breeze,
Nature wakes up, joyful and free.

Birds chime in, a cheerful song,
Harmony where hearts belong.
Morning whispers sweet delight,
With every hue, the world feels right.

Leaves shimmer under gentle light,
Dewdrops glisten, pure and bright.
Children play with gleeful shouts,
In this magic, joy sprouts out.

Together we embrace the dawn,
As colors blend, new dreams are drawn.
In every shade a story told,
A canvas wide, a heart of gold.

A Glimmering Prelude to Day

Morning breaks with golden grace,
A shy embrace, a sweet embrace.
Stars fade softly from the sky,
As rosy hues begin to vie.

The world awakens, fresh and bright,
With laughter echoing sheer delight.
Every corner, vibrant, alive,
In this moment, dreams revive.

Joyous hearts in rhythmic dance,
In the sunlight, we take a chance.
Cupcakes, balloons, and playful cheer,
As the vibrant day draws near.

Colors clash and laugh out loud,
United we stand, proud and loud.
Our spirits soar, no clouds in sight,
In this wondrous, joyful light.

Beneath the Chromatic Canopy

Beneath the trees, colors collide,
We sway together, side by side.
Petals flutter in a breeze,
Nature's quilt, a vivid tease.

Sun-kissed smiles, bright and fair,
Flowers bloom, perfumed air.
Every laugh a joy expressed,
In this haven, we feel blessed.

Kites fly high, drawing our gaze,
In a tapestry, we blaze.
Hand in hand, we run and spin,
Wrapped in warmth, the day begins.

Sharing stories, laughter twirls,
In this canvas, life unfurls.
Underneath this painted sky,
We celebrate, we laugh, we fly.

Radiance of the Morning Sky

With the dawn, our spirits rise,
A canvas blue, where freedom lies.
Clouds drift by in gentle dance,
In their softness, dreams advance.

Candles flicker, a soft glow,
Bright balloons in colors flow.
Joyous hearts, we spread the cheer,
In every smile, a memory dear.

Twinkling lights in every tree,
Like stars that wink just for me.
In this space of pure delight,
We cherish every moment bright.

A symphony of vibrant views,
The morning brings the freshest hues.
Together, as the sun will rise,
We bask beneath the painted skies.

Night's Silent Reverie

Underneath the twinkling stars,
Whispers dance in cool night air.
Laughter echoes, joy nearby,
Every moment, pure and rare.

Silver moonlight bathes the scene,
Dreamers gather, hearts in tune.
Candles flicker, shadows play,
Magic woven 'neath the moon.

Strings of lights adorn the trees,
Voices mingling, hearts align.
Songs of joy as spirits rise,
In this moment, all is fine.

Time stands still, the world feels light,
Memories wrapped in warmth so sweet.
Underneath the stars that shine,
In this reverie, we meet.

Chasing Ghosts of the Sky

Colors splash as daylight fades,
Kites ascend with children's glee.
Laughter bubbles, sparks ignite,
Chasing dreams, so wild and free.

Breezes carry tales of old,
Stories woven into flight.
With each whisper, hearts behold,
Wonders waiting in the night.

Fireflies dance like tiny stars,
Guiding spirits through the dark.
Footsteps echo, paths unfold,
In this moment, feel the spark.

Chasing dreams 'neath velvet skies,
We let laughter take its course.
With our spirits soaring high,
Celebrate this endless force.

The Brushstrokes of Dawn

Morning breaks with golden light,
Birds awake with songs of cheer.
Nature's canvas, oh so bright,
Each hue whispers, spring is near.

Softly hues blend, pink to blue,
Sunlit laughter fills the air.
Every flower feels it too,
In this dance, we're free from care.

As the morning dew ignites,
Joyful hearts in rhythm bloom.
Colors burst with pure delight,
In every corner, spark and plume.

The day begins, embrace the light,
With each brushstroke, life anew.
In this festive, warm invite,
Celebrate the world with you.

Twilight's Light

Beneath the glow of setting sun,
Whispers fold into the night.
Linger here and let dreams run,
Bathed in twilight's gentle light.

Fire pits spark as shadows dance,
Friends gather, spirits bright.
Every laugh, a fleeting chance,
Memories hold us tight.

Lanterns flicker, warm and bold,
Voices blend in a sweet tune.
Stories shared, both new and old,
Underneath the rising moon.

In this moment, time stands still,
Celebrate the joy we find.
Together here, we feel the thrill,
Endless stories intertwined.

Celestial Lighttracks

Stars twinkle in the sky,
Painting dreams on velvet night.
Laughter echoes through the air,
Joy and wonder everywhere.

Moonbeams dance on silken waves,
Whispers of the night it saves.
Hearts are free, the spirit flies,
Beneath the vast, enchanting skies.

Candles flicker, shadows play,
Time slips gently, fades away.
Each moment sparkles, pure delight,
Under the charm of celestial light.

Together we embrace the glow,
As magic weaves through all we know.
In this festivity, we unite,
Bound by the warmth of endless light.

Ephemeral Colors of the Night

Twilight drapes a soft embrace,
On gentle whispers of the space.
Colors blend in sweet array,
A vibrant dance to end the day.

Fireflies flicker, weaving bright,
As laughter bubbles through the night.
Each breath taken tastes like cheer,
Ephemeral wonders drawing near.

Chasing shadows, hearts take flight,
Underneath the silver light.
Moments captured, forever spun,
In the revelry, we all become one.

With every hue, the world ignites,
Painting joy across our sights.
The night is young, the stars invite,
In ephemeral colors of the night.

The Enchantment of Daybreak

Morning whispers secrets sweet,
As colors merge, the day's heartbeat.
Soft rays stretch with tender grace,
Awakening the world to embrace.

Laughter spills from open doors,
A joyful song, the spirit soars.
With every dawn, we start anew,
The enchantment thrums through all we do.

Fields shimmer in golden hue,
Sunshine brightens every view.
In this magic, hopes arise,
Embraced by the promise of blue skies.

Together hand in hand we stand,
The daybreak's joy, oh, so grand.
Each moment savored as we partake,
In the enchantment of daybreak.

Hues of Hope and Wonder

Rainbows weave through drops of light,
A tapestry of sheer delight.
Each hue casts a hopeful thread,
In a world where dreams are fed.

Children laugh, their spirits bright,
Chasing glimpses of pure delight.
Every shade tells a story clear,
Uniting hearts, we draw near.

The air is filled with cheerful sounds,
As magic blooms on colorful grounds.
In every smile, the wonder flows,
A vivid dance where happiness grows.

Together we sip the painted air,
Embracing the beauty everywhere.
In this festival of life, we say,
Hues of hope and wonder guide our way.

Horizon's Gentle Lullaby

The sun dips low in skies of gold,
As laughter spills from young and old.
The waves hum soft a soothing tune,
While stars peek out, a blanket moon.

Fields of joy where memories play,
Every heart shall dance and sway.
With colors bright, the world's aglow,
A gentle breeze, a soft hello.

Beneath the trees, we gather near,
Sharing tales we hold so dear.
A moment's pause, a joyful sigh,
Together here, we reach the sky.

The horizon sings in hues of cheer,
In this warmth, we hold most dear.
The day may end, but love stays bright,
In Horizon's lullaby of light.

Dreams Beneath the Chasing Lights

In twilight's grasp, a promise glows,
With whispers soft, the evening flows.
The city twinkles, alive with dreams,
As laughter dances in moonlit beams.

We chase the stars, both bold and bright,
With hearts ablaze in the velvet night.
Each dream we weave, a story told,
In colors rich, in dreams so bold.

Beneath the glow, all worries fade,
As friendship blooms in this parade.
Hand in hand, we take our flight,
In the magic of the chasing light.

The night is young, the world's our stage,
With every breath, we turn the page.
In dreams we soar, let spirits rise,
Beneath the vast and starry skies.

Symphony of Twilight Hues

As daylight whispers its sweet farewell,
The twilight sings a vibrant spell.
Colors mingle in a stunning blend,
Promising joy as day may end.

Each note it plays, a heart's delight,
A symphony that sparks the night.
With open arms, we greet the stars,
In this embrace, we'll travel far.

The breeze hums low, the world aglow,
With laughter shared, we ebb and flow.
Together wrapped in this soft light,
A festive mood, our hearts take flight.

In every shade, there lies a song,
A rhythm that makes the spirit strong.
As night unfolds, we'll find our way,
In Symphony of Twilight's play.

Iridescent Moments

In the tapestry of fleeting time,
We find our joy in every rhyme.
Iridescent, shining bright,
Moments captured in pure delight.

With laughter ringing through the air,
Each heartbeat shared, we feel the flare.
In dance and song, we lose our cares,
In every gaze, love's magic stares.

The festivities paint the night,
With colors swirling, hearts take flight.
We treasure every fleeting glance,
In these moments, we begin to dance.

As we embrace this chance to shine,
These iridescent moments are divine.
With joyous spirits, we ignite,
The magic found in our shared light.